PRISONER
IN GERMANY

Peter Doyle

SHIRE PUBLICATIONS

First published in Great Britain in 2008 by Shire Publications Ltd,
Midland House, West Way, Botley, Oxford OX2 0PH, United Kingdom.
443 Park Avenue South, New York, NY 10016, USA.

E-mail: shire@shirebooks.co.uk
www.shirebooks.co.uk

© 2008 Peter Doyle.

A CIP catalogue record for this book is available from the British Library.

Shire Library no. 473
ISBN-13: 978 0 7478 0685 1

Peter Doyle has asserted his right under the Copyright, Designs and Patents Act, 1988, to be identified as the author of this book.

Designed by Ken Vail Graphic Design, Cambridge, UK and typeset in Perpetua and Gill Sans.
Printed in Malta by Gutenberg Press Ltd.

08 09 10 11 12   11 10 9 8 7 6 5 4 3 2

COVER IMAGE
British prisoners behind the wire at Stalag XVIIIA, Wolfsburg.

TITLE PAGE IMAGE
A 'goon tower' reconstructed at the site of Stalag VIIIC at Sagan (Zagan).

CONTENTS PAGE IMAGE
The warning wire at Oflag VIB, Warburg. This camp was the scene of the daring escape known as the 'Warburg Wire Job', which used folding ladders to scale the wire. (Sketch by J. R. Hodgson, from *The Quill*, 1947)

DEDICATION
In loving memory of my parents.

ACKNOWLEDGEMENTS
I am grateful for the help and support of many people in the production of this little volume: Mark Radice of Windfall Films, Larry Babits and Jamie Pringle, who worked with me on our excavation of the Stalag Luft III site in 2003; the late Squadron Leader B.A. 'Jimmy' James RAF, General 'Davy' Jones USAAF and Lt-Col. Charles Huppert USAAF, who I had the honour of working with; Nigel Steel of the IWM/AWM with whom I worked on the IWM's Great Escapes exhibit; Lesley Frater of the Fusilier Museum of Northumberland, and William Bishop, who alerted me to the story of Flying Officer Duncan Black; Renate Lippmann of Colditz for her hospitality; Michael Booker for his experience; and Bella Bennett for tracking down ephemera for me. My family have been a constant support; Julie and James.

Most illustrations are from my collection. Permission has been sought were ever possible to reproduce images, many taken from immediate post-war collections of Kriegie drawings – where this has proven impossible I would be happy to include full acknowledgement. Other photographs, as indicated, as published by the kind permission of the Trustees of the Imperial war Museum, and the Fusilier Museum of Northumberland.

CONTENTS

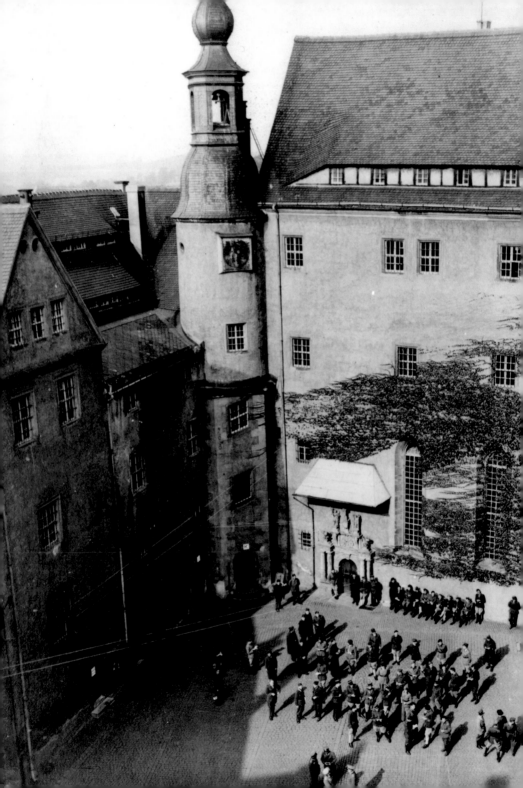

PRISONER OF WAR IN GERMANY, 1939–45

WHAT was it like to be a 'kriegie', a prisoner of war in Germany, during the Second World War? Given the large number of soldiers, sailors and airmen captured, family historians often have photographs of prisoners in the camps, photographs (taken by Germans) that provide perhaps a false impression of shabby comfort, the many hardships hidden. Another common reference point for kriegie life is what one historian has termed the the 'Colditz Myth' – the prevalence of escape stories in books and films. However, there is little to explain what life was like for the average prisoner in Germany. This book provides a simple explanation.

For most prisoners of war (POWs) taken by the Germans in the Second World War, capture came quickly, bewilderingly so in some cases. Surrounded by their enemies, overrun, shot down or sunk, the Allied combatant was to suffer the indignity of surrender to an enemy that, in 1939–41 at least, was in the ascendant. The nations swept up in the Blitzkrieg of 1939–40 were to provide many prisoners; combatants from Poland were first to be incarcerated in POW camps up and down the Reich territory, soon to be joined by Belgian, French and British soldiers after the fall of France in 1940. The tally of Allied soldiers captured by the Germans grew steadily throughout the war: in the desert campaigns of 1940–3 (and transferred from captivity in Italy in 1943), in the abortive attempts at stemming the Axis tide in Greece and Crete in 1941, in the Dieppe Raid of 1943 and during the invasion of Italy in the same year, and (following D-Day) in Normandy, Arnhem and at the Battle of the Bulge in the winter of 1944–5. In total, 164,000 Commonwealth soldiers, sailors and airmen were to become prisoners in Germany, and 95,000 Americans would be captured, 27,500 of them overrun in Hitler's last desperate gamble in the west in the snow-bound Ardennes.

Allied airmen would be captured as their aircraft were shot down or crashed through engine failure and other mechanical fault. The earliest

Opposite:
Oflag IVC, Colditz
– an officers'
Schloss camp.
Colditz had
confined spaces;
the courtyard
depicted was used
for *Appell* and
activities such as
'stoolball', a game
that had its origins
in the Eton 'wall
game', in which
two teams attempt
to score (in part)
by touching a ball
against a wall.
(IWM HU 20288)

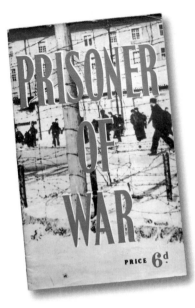

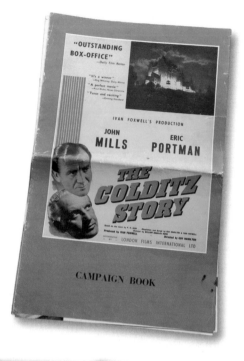

Above left: *Prisoner of War*; c.260,000 British, Commonwealth and American prisoners were captured in Europe and North Africa during the Second World War. This pamphlet was produced by the Red Cross to explain to relatives what they could expect.

Above right: *The Colditz Story*: a publicity campaign book from the premiere of the movie in London on 25 January 1955. Typical of the POW genre movie, it helped create what one historian has termed the 'Colditz Myth' – an idea that kriegie life was centred on escape.

Right: Postcard sent in 1939 by one of the earliest Polish occupants of Oflag IVC, Colditz, surrounded by the image of the imposing castle on German picture postcards. Poles were the first soldiers to enter the camp.

British (and French) prisoners 'in the bag' on the beaches of Dunkirk in May–June 1940. Most would spend five long years in POW camps across Germany.

captives would be those shot down in the Battles for France and on the early abortive bombing missions in inadequate aircraft, no match for German fighters. With the fall of France, the conclusion of the Battle of Britain, and the German aerial blitz on British cities, came the call for bomber fleets to carry the battle to Germany. Losses were high; for RAF Bomber Command 55,000 aircrew would be killed (40 per cent of the total strength) with only 9,838 (8 per cent) surviving to become prisoners of war. For the American Air Force (USAAF), in the 8th Air Force alone 26,000 airmen would be killed and 23,000 captured. In the Battle of the Atlantic the dominance of U-boat warfare meant that the losses were high; over 3,500 Allied merchant ships sunk, and over 30,000 seamen lost – the majority killed.

Although surrender in the heat of battle could be extremely risky, in most cases, surrender would be accepted by the Germans within the bounds

" For you the war is over."

'For you the war is over' – a phrase seemingly uttered by most Germans when taking their prisoners into captivity. (Sketch by R. Anderson, from *Handle With Care*, 1946)

of mutual respect shown by fellow front-line troops. Not so at Wormhout in 1940 and at Malmedy in 1944 when freshly captured prisoners were gunned down in cold blood. As the war in the air intensified, so the safety of Allied aircrew, dubbed '*terror-fliegers*' by the Nazi regime, would suffer the wrath of the local population. Men and women of the special forces were similarly to receive short shrift by the Nazis in the wake of Hitler's 'Commando Order' (Kommandobefehl) of 1942. Commandos and personnel of the Special Operations Executive (SOE) were to be handed over to the Gestapo and executed in concentration camps.

Capture was often proudly met with the phrase (spoken in English), 'For you the war is over' (appearing too often in prisoners' memoirs to be simply a Hollywood cliché). Following capture, on land, at sea or from the air, officers and enlisted other ranks would quickly be separated. Those wounded would receive attention that would range from unbiased treatment of all wounded, through to complete disregard for suffering – a simple lottery based on battle conditions and human frailties. On capture, soldiers could in theory retain their helmets, useful while in the battle zone; all too often they were taken by their captors as souvenirs of battle, inconvenient since they could have served as water containers and soup bowls. Aircrew would find their warm clothing was also prized. These objects would not be the only ones to be 'liberated' from prisoners, as personal items, money, watches and valuables would all too often be taken, sometimes confiscated as war matériel.

In theory the Third Geneva Convention of 1929 would provide universal protection for all prisoners of war. Soviet prisoners were notable exceptions since their government had neither signed nor ratified the treaty; excluded from the care of the Red Cross and the Swiss Protecting Powers, thousands would be starved and worked to death. Nevertheless, the ninety-seven Articles of the Convention laid down principles still in force today: that prisoners of war are entitled to be humanely treated and protected, and not subject to maltreatment or derision, and that they should be evacuated as soon as possible from danger to be interned at prisoner of war camps set up to receive them.

For many men, transit to the POW camp was to rank amongst their most trying times spent in uniform. For those captured en masse on the battlefield, transit would usually involve forced marches away from the front. For the 40,000 British soldiers captured in France during 1940, these marches began in northern France and continued through the Low Countries and into

Germany. Taking many days, marching at a rate of between 15 and 30 miles a day with little formal ration provision, the prisoners became severely undernourished. Begging, scrounging and stealing food from homes and farms, and, as hunger became acute, from each other, is commonly described in prisoners' memoirs. In these early years, with the Nazi regime in the ascendant, there was to be much brutality, with stragglers and those suffering from illness or wounds shown little mercy. Similar conditions were encountered by the 12,000 Commonwealth troops taken prisoner in Greece in 1941, and other difficult marches into captivity were experienced after D-Day, at Arnhem in 1944 and in the Ardennes in 1944–5.

En route, prisoners would enter transit camps (*Durchgangslager* or dulags) – in 1940 very often just open fields with barbed wire, or, at best, tented camps. Finally entering Germany, the marching soldiers were crowded into cattle trucks; any relief that the march was over soon fading with the length of the journey deep into the Reich territory. Stopping infrequently with few ration issues, and locked in for hours on end with no sanitation, the air in the trucks soon became foul.

Dependent on local conditions was the intensity of interrogation, which ranged from standard questioning on the field of battle to complex interrogation in special facilities. Allied aircrew in particular invariably ended up at Dulag Luft at Oberusal, where everything from bogus Red Cross forms to isolation in over-heated cells was employed to extract information. Such ploys were really tried only where there was something to gain: the location of air bases, the number and disposition of troops and ships. But in reality, the average Allied soldier could expect simply to have to give up his name, rank and/or serial number in accordance with Article 5 of the Geneva Convention.

The Geneva Convention also laid down the basic parameters for POW camps. Commonest were the large hutted compounds housing other ranks

Stalag Luft III, Sagan – a hutted compound. An officers' (and NCOs) camp, the huts would be divided into relatively small rooms.
(IWM HU 21013)

The warning wire at Oflag VIB, Warburg. This camp was the scene of the daring escape known as the 'Warburg Wire Job', which used folding ladders to scale the wire. (Sketch by J. R. Hodgson, from *The Quill*, 1947)

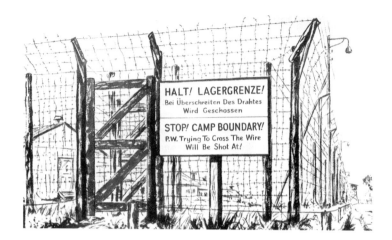

and known as *Stammlagern* or stalags. Officers' camps, *Offizier-lagern* (oflags), were usually more varied in type: from hutted camps to castles and regional palaces pressed into use. The most famous '*Schloss*' (castle) camp was Oflag IVC, based at Colditz in Saxony, a forbidding 900-year-old castle used as a

A 'goon tower' or 'goon box' at an oflag in Germany. (Sketch by Jimmy Graham, from *Joe in Germany*, 1946)

A Luftwaffe guard looks out from a 'goon tower' at Stalag Luft III. A well-known photograph, from the album of the camp commandant. The continental winters could be severe for both prisoners and guards alike. (IWM HU 210270)

Sonderlager, or special camp, for committed escapers and 'enemies of Germany'. Air-force personnel would be housed in hutted compounds (*Stammlagern-Luftwaffe* or stalag lufts) specially constructed on the orders of Reichsmarschall Hermann Goering and run by the Luftwaffe for captured Allied airmen. These compounds grew progressively throughout the war, the most famous being Stalag Luft III, at Sagan in Silesia, scene of the 'Great Escape' in 1944. Naval personnel were held throughout the Reich in a wide variety of camps, as well as in the special Kriegsmarine-run camp (*Marine-Lager*) at Westertimpe, with two adjacent compounds, Marlag (O) for officers, and Marlag (M) for other ranks. Merchant seamen would be interned as civilian prisoners at the adjacent Milag (*Marine-internierten-lager*).

Hutted camps were usually surrounded by a double barbed-wire fence 8 feet high with coiled wire at its centre. The wire itself was thick with fierce, unforgiving barbs, and a low-level warning wire was placed some feet in front of the fence, providing an exclusion zone to inquisitive POWs intent on probing the wire. The wire would be patrolled by soldiers on foot, sometimes with dogs, and observation towers with static guards would be placed at strategic points to cover the wire. Out of humorous contempt for their captors, the prisoners universally referred to the Germans as 'goons', based on the large stupid characters in the 'Popeye' cartoon strip. As guards based in 'goon towers' were armed with machine guns, crossing the warning wire without permission would be courting death.

In the stalags, huts would be divided into large barrack rooms for hundreds of men; for officers these would be smaller, often shared by men in single numbers. Bunks would be hard, often three tier, and sometimes arranged in blocks – in the stalags it was not uncommon to have three-tier bunks arranged in squares of thirty-six. With that many people getting up at

Archaeological remains of the forbidding barbed wire that formed the western boundary of the North Compound of Stalag Luft III, the scene of the 'Great Escape' in March 1944.

MAP OF THE PRINCIPAL CAMPS
FOR BRITISH & DOMINION PRISONERS OF WAR IN EUROPE
PUBLISHED BY
THE RED CROSS & ST. JOHN WAR ORGANISATION

Extract from a map of POW camps produced for relatives by the Red Cross. This one, produced in September 1944, was for British and Commonwealth prisoners; similar ones were published for American prisoners.

intervals through the night to use the cans that acted as toilets, sleep was hard. Palliasse mattresses were supported by wooden bed boards, all too often removed for fuel or use in escape attempts. Heating was invariably from wood-burning stoves; fuel shortages were to become acute in severe winters, and scavenging for wood was prevalent. Washing facilities were basic, with sanitation based usually on communal stalls connected to cesspits that were periodically pumped out into horse-drawn tanks usually referred to by the kriegies as 'honey wagons'.

Camps were numbered according to military district, or *Wehrkreis*, of which there were seventeen at the start of the Second World War, each assigned a roman numeral. Camps in each district would all bear the same numeral, but would be differentiated individually by a letter of the alphabet, as well as by type (oflag, stalag and so on), and would also usually have attached the name of the local town or village. Later, camps would be

Stalag VIIIB, Lamsdorf. The interior of one of the huts, kitted out with three-tier bunks, and decorated for Christmas. Choosing a bunk was a serious business. Those on the lower bunk would be coldest; the centre bunk was dark, and used as a step for those getting to the top; those on the top bunk were often cramped. (IWM HU 23402)

more simply numbered as the system became overloaded. Because of the confined space in commandeered buildings used as officers' camps, subcamps were often set up, denoted by the letter 'Z' (for *Zweiglager*), the main camp being distinguished by 'H', or *Hauptlager*. The most famous example of this was Spangenberg Castle in North Hessen (Oflag IXA/H), and its hutted subcamp set up at nearby Rotenburg (Oflag IXA/Z).

Wehrkreis VIII in Silesia at the eastern margin of Germany was to have most camps. There would be: six stalags A–F (including the infamous Stalag VIIIB, later Stalag 344, at Lamsdorf, one of the largest camps for other ranks), four of which would contain Commonwealth and American troops; nine oflags (including one subcamp); and three stalag lufts, including one initiated as a separate compound in the centre of Stalag VIIIB. There would also be very many workcamps or *Arbeitskommandos* set up as satellites to the main stalags, numbered according to nationality. For example Stalag VIIIB E1 was Arbeitskommando 1 for British Commonwealth troops (men simply lumped together as *Englanders*); it was based at Laband and under the administrative control of the main camps at Lamsdorf.

For men of all camps, survival was to be their primary aim.

An officer's room in Oflag VIIB, Eichstätt, with two-tier bunks and a wood-burning stove converted by the 'tin bashers' into an oven. (Sketch by Jimmy Graham, from *Joe in Germany*, 1946)

THE Prisoner of War

THE OFFICIAL JOURNAL OF THE PRISONERS OF WAR DEPARTMENT OF THE
RED CROSS AND ST. JOHN WAR ORGANISATION, ST. JAMES'S PALACE, LONDON, S.W.1

Vol. 2. No. 19   Free to Next of Kin   November, 1943

The Editor Writes —

THE position as regards prisoners who were until lately in Italian hands is still, to some extent, obscure. Names have been received of a certain number who have escaped into Switzerland. Instructions have been sent to their relatives about the despatch of letters. No parcels can be sent them. Others have been transferred from P.G.19 and other camps to Stalag VII-A, near Munich. Some of them have written home from there saying that this will not be their permanent address. Next of kin parcels should in no case be sent to them until their prisoner of war numbers are known.

Some Have Got Through

It is known from letters that have been received by their relatives and from other sources that a certain number of men have succeeded in filtering through to the British lines and have rejoined their units. In many of the prison camps, however, the Germans took control immediately the armistice was signed and escape was impossible. The Secretary of State for War has told the House of Commons that he is afraid that the bulk of British prisoners who were in Italy are now in Germany or in German hands.

Far East Prisoners

Excellent progress has been made at the Washington Conference of representatives of the British, Canadian and U.S. Red Cross Societies. Unanimous decisions were arrived at and a concerted approach has been made to the Japanese authorities with a view to getting them to discharge their obligations to their prisoners of war. The British Red Cross Mission is remaining in America and is continuing joint consultations on the building

up and carrying out of effective plans. But everything still depends on the attitude of the Japanese Government. Details will be found on page 14.

Red Cross Supplies

In certain individual cases it is known that Red Cross supplies have been received, and I have before me a letter from a delighted wife at Keighley (Yorks), whose husband in Taiwan Camp, Formosa Island, reports the "arrival of Red Cross relief goods." She says: "This news has made us all happy." Another card, from a naval signalman, informs his

mother at Retford that he is safe and well in Fukuoka No. 2 Camp.

From a Jersey Septuagenarian

Miss Marjorie Wick, of Golders Green, sends us a letter she has had from her 70-year-old Uncle Jim, who has been taken from Jersey to Ilag VII. He says: "I feel fine, and making the best of it—peeling potatoes, washing tins, sweeping yards, water 'carrying and carrying' down the empty Red Cross tins from our room." They have a good library and concerts, etc., at intervals, and he mentions that he is going to visit a patient in an outside hospital—"a nice change." There was some talk of all over 60 going home, but——"the railroads are all upset and travelling is very awkward."

British Morale

Here is an extract from a letter written to his wife, Mrs. Edna Knight, of Epsom, by a private in a Stalag who has been put in charge of sports and is being kept very busy. "You see, dear," he says, "in this life somebody must take charge of these things; it keeps these poor boys occupied and gives them less time to think. It is up to us who have been soldiers for years to do what we can for them. But they are British, and that is everything. The morale here is wonderful." The writer of this letter is 31, has been a prisoner since May, 1940, has had one-leg amputated, lost the use of his left arm (he was left-handed) and had eight bomb wounds in his back.

Acknowledgments

Among many others who have written me recently to express grateful thanks for the work of the Red Cross

Members of the R.A.F. at Stalag Luft 3.

'KRIEGIE' LIFE – SURVIVING

O N arrival at one of the main camps, prisoners would be processed, formally entering Wehrmacht records for the first time. From this point on the prisoners would use the term 'kriegie' to describe themselves, derived from the German for POW, *Kriegsgefangener*. Typically, kriegies would be shorn of their hair and deloused; they would be photographed and fingerprinted for their registration cards, and be issued with a *Kriegsgefangener* number and rectangular identification disc. A postcard would also be issued for prisoners to notify their families that they were safe and let them know the location of their POW camp

That Germany was a signatory to the Geneva Convention ensured, in name, that prisoners were fed and clothed; yet the inadequacy of the German provision was to force governments and the International Red Cross to supply food parcels and clothing for captured Allied combatants. For the prisoners of 1940–1, clothing issue depended largely upon stocks of captured uniforms. This could mean that the average POW could expect to be wearing the remains of his own uniform, together, perhaps, with poorly fitting French trousers, a Belgian overcoat, a Polish cap, *fusslappen* (cloth rags wrapped around the feet in place of socks), and wooden sabots or clogs. This miscellany of captured items would eventually be replaced by uniforms sent from home from 1941–2 onwards.

According to Article 11 of the Convention, the Germans were expected to supply rations that would be equivalent in quantity and calorific value to those given to their own depot troops. This was far from the truth. For example, those prisoners arriving at Stalag VIIIB (Lamsdorf) in 1940 would receive only: ersatz coffee (made from acorns) or mint 'tea' for breakfast; a ladleful of weak soup and two or three, often rotten, potatoes at midday; followed by a third of a loaf of bread in the evenings. Soup was the staple in all camps; some cooks would grace the thin greasy liquid with titles intended to conjure up images of hearty meals, such as vegetable soup and goulash stew. Despite this, the dish never varied, and consisted of a watery concoction containing a few small bones, some vegetable stalks, a shred or two of meat

Opposite:
The Prisoner of War
– a magazine produced by the Red Cross for free distribution to the families of British POWs; the American Red Cross produced its *Prisoner of War Bulletin* with the same aim in mind. Both did a good job, but in some cases promoted an over-rosy view of actual conditions.

The remains of a plimsoll shoe at Stalag Luft III; the wear marks indicate that this large-sized shoe was worn by a man with a much smaller shoe size. Kriegies would press into service anything that was comfortable and easy to wear.

Right: Wooden cutlery made by a prisoner in Stalag Luft VI, Heydedrug. As soup was the main ration item, only the spoon has seen use.

Above: POW identity tag marked with both the camp and the individual's numbers. The tag was worn around the neck, suspended from a cord. This one is from Stalag VIIIA, Görlitz, where 2,500 British Commonwealth and 1,800 American prisoners were incarcerated, together with men of other Allied nations.

Group of British prisoners from the Royal Engineers at Stalag XVIIIA, Wolfsburg, in south-east Austria; their uniforms were supplied direct from the UK, replacing the miscellany of rag-tag uniform scraps from many nations originally issued by the Germans.

and an occasional potato. It is not surprising that in the early days and later, when the supply line for the Red Cross broke down during the onslaught on Germany, it was the dark rye bread (comprising around 30 per cent sawdust and straw) that was the only substantial component of this meal.

Shared between three men, who gathered in 'syndicates' or 'combines', the ration bread would be cut with utmost care. Some prisoners used the width of the metal POW tag as a guide to thickness, others would observe the act of cutting with fanatical attention to detail, such was the importance of the act. Deciding who would get which piece was also fraught with difficulties: sometimes it would be by the cutting of cards, in others cases, the bread cutter would take the last piece to ensure he maintained a steady hand. Arguments would frequently break out, and syndicates break up over the smallest irregularities in the ritual cutting. The bread ration would also be a test of the personal traits of the individual, and two main types appeared: 'hoarders' and 'bashers'. Hoarders would save at least part of their bread ration to have as breakfast with the unwholesome coffee issue; bashers would eat theirs there and then and go hungry later. This behaviour would be replicated when Red Cross parcels started to arrive in the camps.

Food parcels were sent by all the free nations under the auspices of the International Red Cross, and the vast majority of kriegie memoirs pay homage to their life-sustaining qualities. Prisoners from the Commonwealth and the USA would receive parcels packed in their own countries, but the

British Red Cross parcel – similar parcels were supplied from the USA and all the Commonwealth countries.

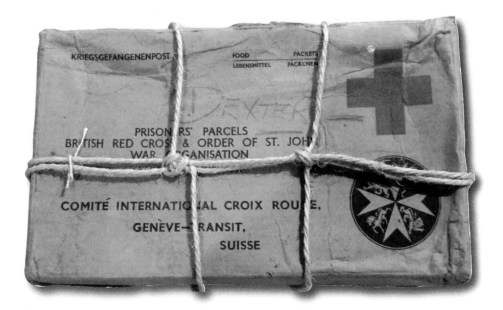

Contents of a
Canadian Red Cross
parcel. (Sketch by
John Worsley, from
Only Ghosts Can Live,
1945)

Below: The typical
content of Red
Cross parcels.
Compiled from *Joe in
Germany* (1947), *Only
Ghosts Can Live*
(1945), *Aben Caplan's
POW Diary* (Library
of Congress) and
*Prisoner of War My
Secret Journal* (1988)

Canadian	British	American
Corned beef (12 oz can)	Meat and vegetables (16 oz can)	Spam (16 oz can)
Pork roll (10 oz can)	Bacon (7 oz can)	Corned beef (16 oz can)
Salmon (7½ oz can)	Meat roll (10 oz can)	Liver paste (6 oz can)
Sardines (5¼ oz can)	Salmon (7½ oz can)	Tuna or salmon (8 oz can)
Jam (16 oz can)	Oats (5 oz packet)	Jam (8 oz can)
Cheese (4 oz can)	Cheese (3 oz can)	Cheese (8 oz can)
Biscuits (16 oz)	Service biscuits (8 oz packet)	Crackers (one packet)
Chocolate (6 oz)	Chocolate (4 oz)	Chocolate (16 oz)
Tea (4 oz packet)	Tea (2 oz packet)	Coffee (2 oz can)
Dried milk 'Klim' (16 oz tin)	Cocoa (4 oz)	Cocoa (one can)
Sugar (4 oz)	Condensed milk (12 oz can)	Dried milk (16 oz tin)
Raisins (7 oz packet)	Sugar (4 oz block)	Sugar (8 oz packet)
Prunes (6 oz packet)	Raisins (8 oz packet)	Raisins/prunes (16 oz)
Butter 'Maple Leaf' (16 oz can)	Margarine (8 oz can)	Margarine (16 oz can)
Packet of salt and pepper	Packet of pudding mixture	Vitamin tablets (box of 12)
Tablet of soap	Dried egg (2 oz can)	Two tablets of soap
	Tablet of soap	
50 cigarettes supplied in a separate tin		100 cigarettes in five packs

Prisoners unpacking Canadian Red Cross parcels at Stalag VIIIB, Lamsdorf. Both 'Klim' (milk spelt backwards) powdered milk (380 calories) and 'Maple Leaf Creamery Butter' (486 calories) would be major supplements to the kriegies' diet, and together be an important source of vitamins A and D. One of the butter tins has been transformed into a mug with the addition of a handle. (IWM HU 23441)

issue would vary, such that an American prisoner might expect to receive parcels packed in the USA, Britain, Canada and so on. Weighing around 11 pounds, the parcels contained mostly canned and dry goods that would survive storage and transportation, and that were intended to provide food components missing from the German ration, the dried milk, butter and

Volunteers packing parcels for the American Red Cross. Some 13,500 volunteers assembled the packages in packing centres in New York, Philadelphia, Chicago and St Louis. (Library of Congress)

Right: The 'Penny a Week' fund was an initiative to raise funds – literally a penny a week – for the British Red Cross and St John War Organisation.

Far right: Poster issued to raise funds for parcels and other POW support from the War Organisation of the Red Cross and St John in the UK. Stalag XVIIIA, Wolfsburg, depicted on the poster housed over 10,000 British and Commonwealth prisoners.

cheese in particular providing missing nutrients. Prisoners would come to rely on the parcels, which contained around 2,070 calories, 63 per cent of the 3,300 daily total required by working men. Parcels were issued at the rate of one per man, per week, though it was usual for men in syndicates to combine their parcels to gain variety.

From Britain alone, twenty million food parcels were delivered by eight ships that kept up a constant shuttle service between the UK, Lisbon in neutral Portugal, and Marseilles in the south of France. From there, the parcels were delivered by post to the International Committee of the Red Cross in Geneva, who distributed them to the POW camps. These parcels were packed at seventeen centres across Britain, staffed by volunteers from the Red Cross and St John War Organisation, who produced up to 163,000

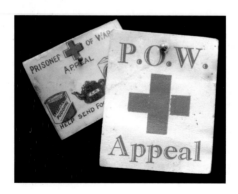

Australian Red Cross charity 'flags' used to raise funds for POWs.

parcels a week. The American Red Cross prepared and shipped twenty-seven million parcels, with some 13,500 volunteers assembling the packages in packing centres in New York, Philadelphia, Chicago and St Louis. Payment for the parcels in both countries was through charity. In the UK, the 'Penny a Week' fund was set up to fund the Red Cross and St John War Organisation by the collection of regular small payments off the doorstep and in workplaces. The scheme was highly successful; similar fund-raising drives were held in other countries to provide funds for this massive undertaking.

The issue of Red Cross parcels from late 1940 onwards was to alleviate the hunger felt by most prisoners in the early days of the war. In the main, the Germans handed on parcels without interference, but in some cases antagonistic commandants would order tin cans to be pierced or even the contents of the tins and packets to be emptied into one bowl – ostensibly to prevent hoarding as escape food. Parcels would also be withheld as reprisals in some cases. The hunger of 1940–1 was to reappear in 1944–5 when the normal supply of parcels was interrupted as the Allies pushed into Germany. Fortunately, the International Committee of the Red Cross, recognising real danger of starvation, organised the convoys that were to become known to the prisoners as 'White Angels' – fleets of white-painted trucks with prominent red crosses that were able to reach most camps across Germany – and particularly those closest to the advancing Red Army.

Red Cross parcels had other uses beyond the simple provision of life-sustaining food. The wooden packing cases that contained the cardboard boxes on delivery were used for larger construction efforts: the manufacture of comfortable chairs or, most famously, the

Above: 'Maple Leaf Creamery Butter' tin from a Canadian Red Cross parcel made into a jug by the addition of a handle. (With kind permission of the Fusilier Museum of Northumberland)

Below: Lt-Col Charles Huppert USAAF, a 'tin-basher' at Stalag Luft III, Sagan, demonstrates his skills to a modern audience. Charles learned how to make do as a farm boy in Indiana.

'Blowers' were fan-assisted ovens made from Klim tins, which maximised heat output through a system of gears. These could be fearsome and used the minimum of fuel; they were the preferred method of cooking and making 'brews'. (Sketch by R. Anderson, from *Handle With Care*, 1946)

sides of the wooden vaulting horse used to hide an escape tunnel in Stalag Luft III in 1943. Scrap wood was also used for fuel in the severe winters of continental Europe, essential to undernourished men. Finally, tin cans provided ample opportunity for inventiveness by the 'tin-bashers'. 'Tin bashing' provided a useful pastime and allowed those practically minded to create a range of gadgets and utensils. At the simplest level, tins could be fashioned into cups and plates; at the more complex, they could be combined to form Heath-Robinsonesque contraptions called 'blowers' (or 'stufas'). Blowers were created from the tin-basher's favourite – the 'Klim' tin – which was wide and squat, just perfect for the manufacture of a portable stove or water boiler. Using a series of wheel-driven fans, Klim-tin blowers could boil water in double-quick time, using the smallest amount of fuel possible. Cans also had many applications in escape tunnels, the most famous being the ventilation tubes created for the tunnels 'Tom', 'Dick' and 'Harry' for the Great Escape from Stalag Luft III in 1944.

With smoking part of everyday life in the 1940s, the provision of cigarettes and tobacco to POWs was of paramount importance. The British

Far left: 'Klim' – the powdered milk included in most Canadian Red Cross parcels. The 4 inch wide tin was suitable for a range of 'tin-bashing' activities.

Left: Wartime tin of fifty 'Gold Flake' cigarettes; similar tins were supplied to prisoners through the Red Cross. The cigarette soon became the only acceptable camp currency.

and Canadian Red Cross supplied each man with fifty cigarettes, usually in tins, the American one hundred cigarettes being issued in five packs. More came from home and regimental 'comfort funds'. In much shorter supply were matches and lighters.

Largely unavailable in Nazi Germany, the Virginian cigarette assumed an importance way beyond that normally associated with it, quickly becoming the hard currency of the camps. Cigarettes were the basis of trade with other prisoners, and with their German guards, who would abandon temporarily allegiance to their Führer for the price of a few cigarettes, procuring whatever might be needed to increase kriegie comfort. Cigarettes had a nominal exchange rate: one account, written in 1945, suggests a rate of exchange of between 90 pfennigs to 1 mark 50 pfennigs (a buying power at time of writing of around £1 to £2 , or $2 to $4). Financially astute prisoners soon amassed cigarette fortunes. Non-smokers had the advantage as they still

'Rackets'. Stalls with objects for sale would appear in many camps – here depicted at Stalag 383, Hohenfels. Cigarettes were the only currency accepted. (Sketch by A. G. Dallimore, from Barbed Wire, 1947)

Below left: Packing lists for quarterly 'personal parcels' sent to Gunner Anthony Harrison in Stalag XXA, Thorn, from his family, via the Red Cross. Parcels were to include toiletries and clothing items; the 'treasure bag' was a small drawstring bag home-made to Red Cross specification.

Below right: Standard postcards sent from Stalag VIIIB, Lamsdorf, by British and American prisoners. Both bear the standard censor stamps (Geprüft – examined).

obtained their ration; but commercially minded individuals were to create a system of trade (Geschäft) or 'rackets' that at worst could see prisoners trading food for cigarettes, though many other articles were on sale. In many cases the rackets were run openly, with stalls set up in the hutted camps; basic barter was also available through numerous 'swap shops' that also sprang up.

In addition to food parcels, Allied Red Cross organisations carried responsibility for liaising with the relatives of POWs. Magazines and bulletins were produced and issued free to relatives; these carried letters from prisoners, titbits of sometimes over-rosy information about individual camps, and advice to family members. Particularly important to the kriegies themselves were the quarterly personal parcels sent from home, packed according to the advice of the Red Cross. Sent through the auspices of the International Red Cross, these were to weigh around 10 pounds, and were to contain no foodstuffs (other than chocolate), concentrating on clothing, stationery, toiletries and the ubiquitous cigarettes and tobacco. Books and games could also be sent, also via the Red Cross, from wholesalers; newspapers and magazines were, however, forbidden.

The receipt of letters was of the greatest significance to prisoners and families alike – with delayed mail causing particular heartache. For their part, the Germans issued four postcards and two standard letter-forms a month for the use of each prisoner; surviving examples provide unique snapshots of kriegie life. Each item of correspondence from POW camps was censored and bears a camp censor mark (Geprüft – examined), with each item sent

Letter-forms produced for relatives writing to POWs in Germany; British and American versions are similar. For British captives at least, 'keep your chin up' was a popular opener. All letters sent to POW camps were subject to scrutiny by Allied censors.

from home also scrutinised – by Allied censors. While most correspondence from home expressed the hope that prisoners were 'keeping their chins up' (a standing kriegie joke), not all mail would be as encouraging. Photographs taken by the Germans, made available to prisoners and regularly sent home, promoted a kind of 'holiday camp' illusion that belied the real hardships of POW life. One RAF sergeant in Stalag Luft VI was to receive this card in 1944: 'Sorry you liked the scarf. I had hoped it would have gone to someone on Active Service.' Such sentiments were by no means atypical. Infamous also were the letters from wives and sweethearts informing their men that they had tired of waiting and had left them for another. Such devastating news could have desperate effects on prisoner morale; offending letters would be pinned up by bitter prisoners for all to see.

'KRIEGIE' LIFE –
APPELL AND *ARBEIT*

A N average day at an average camp would begin at around 6 a.m., when German guards would attempt to raise the kriegies with cries of *Raus* (out), lights on and whistles. Breakfast would follow, the preferred option being tea from Red Cross parcels – German ersatz acorn coffee or mint 'tea' fetched from the cookhouse was generally a last resort. Tea would be taken with any ration bread left over from the day before, together with any remaining jam and margarine from a Red Cross parcel.

Appell followed, a rollcall parade to audit the numbers of prisoners present, and a means of public announcement by the commandant. Some men simply avoided it, staying in their bunks; others, already counted, tricked the guards by 'increasing' the number of men on parade, running behind the back of the front rank to bolster numbers. Contempt for the arithmetical skills of the 'goons' was widespread. This would infuriate the German officers and would form part of a long-running pastime usually referred to as 'goon baiting'. *Appell* could last for at least an hour, and there could be as many as three rollcalls a day in some camps.

From about 8 o'clock onwards, huts would be cleaned by those detailed as 'orderlies', and others would do their best to clean themselves from the few taps that actually worked. Working parties would assemble to be taken out of the compound, while others would engage in a miscellany of activities, from sport to education. Ration soup would be served at around 11; some prisoners would be more inclined to eat from their Red Cross parcels much later in the day. Officially, this food would have to be taken to the cookhouse; mostly it was cooked privately using one of the many blowers and 'patent cookers' made by the tin-bashers.

Afternoons would be spent as best they could be in a range of activities, from trading to attending lectures; workers (or *Arbeiters*) would have little chance to engage in such things. In the evening there would be trips to the camp theatre, tickets (printed on scrap card) fairly allotted in turn to portions

Opposite:
Army other ranks at work in one of the many workcamps (*Arbeitskommandos*) administered by Stalag VIIIB, Lamsdorf. (IWM HU 9212)

of the camp. Lights would go out at 10 p.m. after a 'final brew' if the Red Cross parcels could sustain it.

Communication with the German commandant was through a small staff of senior prisoners who would negotiate for the welfare of their charges, and who would have to invoke on a regular basis the Articles of the Geneva Convention. In officers' camps the POWs would be led by the appropriate senior officer; in the case of the Anglophone Allies this could be the most senior officer between them or, where separately housed, the Senior British

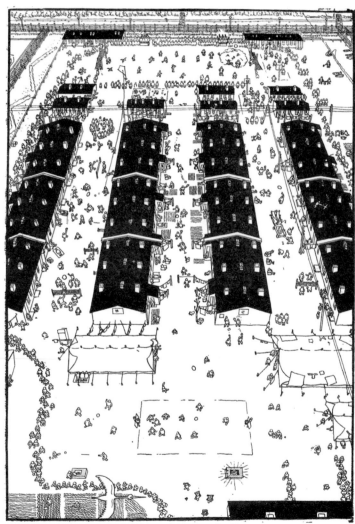

Privacy was a problem in all camps – especially so as more and more prisoners were captured as the war progressed. (Sketch by R. Anderson, from *Handle With Care*, 1946)

"I just want to be alone"

Manacles – these were worn by NCO prisoners in reprisal for the order instructing Canadian troops to bind German prisoners at Dieppe. Very often these manacles could be removed through the judicious application of a sardine-tin key.

Officer (SBO) or Senior American Officer (SAO). In the stalags, a senior NCO would be elected by the men to represent them as their 'Man of Confidence'. Other members of the staff would be German-speaking prisoners to act as interpreters. Medical officers and corpsmen, also POWs, would complete the entourage.

Following the abortive raid at Dieppe in August 1942, when a copy of the detailed military plan for the raid fell into enemy hands, a series of reprisals was carried out against prisoners of war. The Dieppe plan included recommendations for the binding of any POWs captured (to prevent the disposal of valuable documents), an unfortunate fact exacerbated by a case of POW binding by commando troops raiding the Channel Island of Sark. The German response was immediate and severe, with around a thousand or so officers and NCOs initially bound with cord (from Red Cross parcels) as a reprisal. This number was to rise to many thousands of NCOs shackled and manacled in camps across Germany. This act, though inconvenient, was later to become an embarrassment to the Germans, as by 1944 guards resorted to simply issuing the manacles to the prisoners after morning *Appell* and collecting them in the evening. Prisoners had, in any case, realised that the manacles could be removed through the judicious use of a sardine-tin key. The shackling episode became one more aspect of camp life to be endured.

Mental and physical stagnation was feared by the predominantly young prisoner population, and most found it essential to engage in activities that would allow them to escape the grey drudgery and squalor of the POW camp. The activities available varied from camp to camp, and particularly so between officers' and other ranks' camps. By the Articles of the Geneva Convention, officers were not required to work (unless volunteering to do so), and NCOs could work only in a supervisory role. Air-force personnel were barred from work altogether for fear of them escaping; new aircrew took a long time to train. Many NCOs refused to work, driven by motives as diverse as patriotic duty through to laziness and ambivalence to hard labour. A special *Sonderlager*, Stalag 383, was set up at Hohenfels in Bavaria to house these non-working NCOs, some of whom were 'self promoted' in order to avoid the work details. Private soldiers had no choice but to work.

For the average private, the only choice available would be to volunteer for one type of working party or another in the hope that conditions and food might be better. For a camp like Stalag VIIIB at Lamsdorf, containing tens of thousands of men from Britain, the Commonwealth and the USA, there would be hundreds of satellite workcamps spread out over Silesia. Although the main camp would be responsible for the distribution of parcels and mail, each *Arbeitskommando* acted as a self-contained subcamp. These workcamps would vary in quality, and could include everything from a self-contained and newly built hutted camp through to industrial premises.

Work would be long and hard, and included labouring in the fields and factories, construction work and mining. In the main, and where he could get away with it, the Allied POW adopted a studied incompetence in order to avoid the hardest work. There were some compensations to work, however: in some rare cases the food issue was better, and there was the opportunity to fraternise with the locals, trading cigarettes for contraband items such as fresh eggs, particularly where *Arbeitskommandos* operated in Polish territory. Here there was also the possibility of liaisons with local women, even though these were strictly forbidden by the Nazi regime.

All men would receive pay in *Lagergeld* or *Lagermarks*, slips of paper that had no value outside the camp, and little value within it. Officers' pay was theoretically redeemable from the British or American governments, as it was issued in lieu of their service pay. In the early days of the war, up to 1942, pay could be exchanged for items in the German-run 'canteens'; these included ersatz soap, ersatz soup powders, ersatz cigarettes – all as useless as the *Lagermarks* themselves. After 1942, there would be little to spend these on. In fact, these worthless pieces of paper, printed in several denominations, were largely used as gambling tokens, the real currency of the markets being the cigarette.

When not working, prisoners would engage in a variety of pastimes, tin-bashing, already mentioned, being one of them. Another was 'goon baiting', collective aggravation of the German guards that started at *Appell* and ran through the day at a low level. Everything from practical jokes, feigning deafness and a chronic lack of understanding of German orders was tried.

Lagergeld or *Lagermarks* – camp currency paid to the kriegies. Largely worthless, these notes usually ended up being used as tokens in gambling.

The cry of 'Goon up!' was to be heard whenever a German entered a hut, tolerated by some commandants, clamped down upon by others. The 'goons' themselves were always vigilant in case any act of the kriegies could be seen to be openly mocking them. In some cases, when German tolerance was tested by POWs sailing close to the wind; senior officers had to intervene to prevent bloodshed.

Sport was extremely important to the morale of the prisoners, and the commonest activities included athletics in the summer months through to cricket, softball, football (soccer), field hockey and rugby. In the coldest winters, ice-skating was also a common pastime. The redoubtable Red Cross gathered the funds to provide the sports equipment and produced crates containing a diversity of balls, sticks, bats, nets and boxing gloves designed to cater for the sporting needs of one hundred men. In addition, thirty complete sports strips were sent with the crates, while the YMCA supplied boots through Geneva. Mini-Olympics, World Cups and World Series were played out on the sports fields of most large camps, while in *Sonderlagern* like Oflag IVC (Colditz), new sports such as 'stoolball', which involved charging at a prisoner on a stool holding a ball, had to be devised for its enclosed courtyards. At Stalag Luft III, golf balls and sticks were painstakingly constructed. For many at home a view prevailed, fuelled by over-rosy portraits of camp life in Red Cross literature, that POW life was a sporting paradise. Nothing could be further from the truth.

Education ranked highly on the list of activities and, given the mix of civilian backgrounds, there were always enough experts to lecture on a range of subjects. Camp 'universities', providing instruction in examinations

'The first football match in EI'. Football and other sports were extremely popular in all POW camps; this one was organised in *Arbeitskommando* EI, Stalag VIIIB, in 1942, before the issue of Red Cross football kits and YMCA football boots.

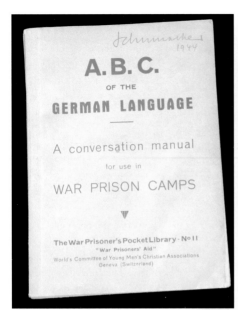

Above left: Learning German as a pursuit had many advantages – enabling the prisoners to communicate with their guards (and therefore to indulge in trade), or to be used on escape. This phrasebook was produced for Allied prisoners by the YMCA and has a camp censor mark.

Above right: *The Camp* – a German news-sheet produced in English that was circulated throughout the camps. It contained mostly low-key ineffectual news gleaned from the Allied press, together with the main stories that trumpeted German successes – even when these were few late in the war.

Right: *Here We Are!* – camp magazine ostensibly produced by the prisoners of the 'holiday camp' run as part of Stalag IIID, Berlin. The 'holiday camp' was set up as a German propaganda ploy, and a means of possible recruitment of British and Commonwealth soldiers into the Waffen SS. It was largely unsuccessful on both counts. Many other magazines and wall newspapers would be produced in camps across Germany.

accredited in Britain, were also set up, with Stalag Luft VI having a particularly good reputation – but as one RAF sergeant would report from Luft VI in 1944: 'I'm still managing to keep the old chin up, but, believe me, studying is not the right way of passing time away.'

In the early days of some camps, possession of a book made individual kriegies sought-after individuals, but this pressure abated when camp libraries were built up with the aid of the Red Cross, containing many hundreds of volumes.

Chinese Art – one of the many books on obscure subjects from the library of Stalag VIIIB, Lamsdorf. Those inclined could spend much time in the pursuit of knowledge, however arcane.

Opposite left: The YMCA was to distribute 'logbooks' to all prisoners in order for them to maintain a journal of their experiences; British Commonwealth and American versions were produced. The American version was larger, with the Liberty Bell, while the British version had a lion. The British example illustrated was the property of Captain Müller MC of the New Zealand Army Service Corps, incarcerated at Oflag IXA/Z, Rotenburg.

Opposite right: *Backwater* – a collection of literary and artistic pieces from the officer prisoners of Oflag IXA/H, Spangenberg, published (on high-quality paper) in 1944. Many prisoners were committed to cultural pursuits.

This page: Pamphlet recording the successes of prisoners at examinations taken in Stalag Luft VI, Heydekrug, often held up as the 'stalag university'.

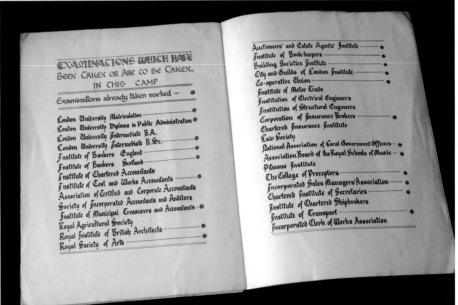

Other reading material included the German-produced newspaper *The Camp*, published in English, which contained low-key 'news' on German military successes and Allied failures, together with titbits garnered from home newspapers, including sports results. Prisoners resorted to producing their own newsletters and bulletins, often to quash rumours ('griff'), and posted these on hut walls. Examples include the *Daily Recco* at the Centre Compound of Stalag Luft III, and *Stimmt* and *The Clarion* at Stalag VIIIB. These rags were partially made up of news gained from the clandestine radio sets smuggled into the camp, usually bought from the guards with cigarettes. In some cases, such as the hand-drawn motoring magazine *Flywheel*, an output of the 'Muhlberg Motor Club' of Stalag IVB, the production of magazines attained a high art. The YMCA was also active in ministering to the prisoners' intellectual needs, and was to issue 'logbooks' to be kept as a journal.

Cultural needs were met with musical instruments, sheet music, play scripts and costumes (issued on parole), again provided mostly through the auspices of the Red Cross in Geneva. Gramophone records would also provide some light relief from the tedium of camp life. Revues, serious plays, musicals, all were catered for, and in some cases prisoners were allowed to construct their own theatres. Big productions would require lighting experts, musicians and actors – with men playing the part of women. In an all-male environment the presence of 'women' in the camp was intoxicating, and in some cases the 'women' actors took their part further in acting as partners in prison-camp dances. For those inclined this provided an outlet for a side of their personality that might be otherwise hidden, and for their admirers it was a way of imagining what it might be like when released back into a world of real women. Not everyone would approve.

Private Mervyn Baker at the piano in *Arbeitskommando* E1, a subcamp of Stalag VIIIB, Lamsdorf. Musical revues and similar entertainments were well received by most prisoners.

Vices, a seamier counterpoint to the cultural side, were prevalent. Gambling was common, involving everything from ludo to snail racing, with cigarettes being the only acceptable stakes. Dice, two-up, crown and anchor, all were used, and in rougher camps gangs of razor-wielding toughs would operate extortion and intimidation. Sex with women was largely impossible, beyond fleeting and dangerous liaisons on working parties. In any case, at times of intense hunger thoughts of such activity faded, to be replaced by other longings, particularly for favourite foods. Kriegies would draw up impossible menus that replaced pin-ups at their bunks. Drinking raw alcohol was more prevalent, with various types of 'hootch' distilled from potatoes and raisins – pure spirit of dubious quality that was all-too-often damaging to the health of the drinker – anything that would help quell the longing for home.

Above left: The costume maker at the camp theatre of Stalag Luft III, Sagan. (IWM HU 21140)

Above right: Private Dennis Merry, female impersonator at *Arbeitskommando* El, a workcamp at Laband under the control of Stalag VIIIB. (IWM HU 9259)

'KRIEGIE' LIFE – CONTRASTS

THE experience of individual prisoners of war in Germany depended rather on their place of capture, their rank, their branch of service, and the location and reputation of their prisoner of war camp. Some aspects never changed: the monotony of the standard German soup and bread diet, the universal gratitude to the International Red Cross, and the developing kriegie slang, a language shared by all. To get some idea of the life of prisoners in Germany, three contrasting personal experiences are described – a soldier captured in 1940, a soldier captured in 1945, and an airman shot down in 1943.

PRIVATE LESLIE DOYLE, KRIEGSGEFANGENER 10111, STALAG VIIIB E1

Leslie Doyle's story is typical of the thousands of young men conscripted into the British army on the eve of the Second World War. Born in 1918 in the northern shipbuilding town of Birkenhead, he was called up to the

Grainy print of Les Doyle (right) and friend at Stalag VIIIB. Such photographs were taken by the Germans to be sent home.

territorial 'militia' during the 'Phoney War' of late 1939, and drafted to the 5th Battalion King's Own (Royal Lancaster) Regiment, part of the Territorial 42nd (East Lancashire) Division. Within months of his call-up, in early April 1940, he was shipped to France with the rest of the British Expeditionary Force (BEF), and by 10 May the 5th King's Own formed part of the defensive line on the River Dyle, digging trenches and improving the position. By 21 May 1940, the BEF had fallen back to the Escaut near Tournai, in the face of the German onslaught. Private Les Doyle's 'D' Company formed the right of the British line at Bourghelles, adjoining the French 8th Zouaves. Coming under direct attack from Stuka dive-bombers, the French retired on 27 May, leaving D Company unprotected. Retreat was the only option. The battalion moved back steadily, forming part of the rearguard to the perimeter of Dunkirk. Les Doyle and other members of his company were separated, and while 300 of his mates were taken off the beaches at Dunkirk by HMS *Locust*, he found himself 'in the bag' on 1 June 1940, captured at Hazebrouck.

In common with all men of the BEF left behind after the withdrawal, Private Doyle faced a trying march through the Low Countries and into Germany. The memories of that journey into Belgium never left him. The German guards, reasonable at first in the flush of victory, soon ran out of

Above left:
Anahof – the now deserted platform where all prisoners arrived in cattle trucks at Stalag VIIIB. Private Les Doyle arrived here in early June 1940.

Above right:
The remains of the only road into Stalag VIIIB, now leading to the forest that covers the site at Lambinowice, Poland.

Above: Postcard sent home from Private Doyle, *Kriegsgefangener* 10111, Stalag VIIIB, in July 1941.

Right: Christmas card for 1941 sent by Les Doyle from Stalag VIIIB. Drawn by one of the prisoners, these were printed by the Germans and issued in place of the usual *Kriegsgefangenpost* cards.

patience with their burdensome captives, particularly the British. (His former French comrades were to receive better treatment.) The journey east was arduous, first on foot and then, once into German territory, crowded into cattle trucks. Given little to sustain life, Les and his mates arrived at the railhead of Stalag VIIIB (Lamsdorf) – Anahof – now a deserted, solitary, low platform on the former Berlin–Breslau railway. From here, marched along a paved road – the only road entering the camp in an otherwise unbroken stretch of barbed wire – they passed by a cemetery of the First World War dead of Stalag VIIIB, and marched into the camp on 10 June 1940. Les Doyle spent the rest of the war as a prisoner.

Stalag VIIIB (renumbered Stalag 344 in 1943) was set up as a POW camp in the First World War, and covered nearly 80 acres of land, with ten compounds of prisoners, a hospital area, and German offices. A typical hutted camp, home to tens of thousands of prisoners, it had a double perimeter fence 8 feet high, with elevated machine-gun posts looking down on the separate compounds. It was a squalid place. Les spent a week at the *Stammlager* before being detailed for an *Arbeitskommando*, E1 at Laband, a large working camp under the administrative control of the stalag. Like other private soldiers, Les was forced to work, doing metal construction work for Siemens, and was left scarred for life when he caught a hot rivet. Many such rivets were partially cut through by the prisoners – a small victory in this war of waiting. Nearby, Soviet prisoners were being worked and starved to death; this sight angered the kriegies (and haunted Les Doyle for the rest of his life), who made intimidating noises to the Russians' guards, and who, in open defiance, threw their unknown allies food and cigarettes.

It was sport that kept Les going, playing for one of the many named football teams, a reminder of home – Tottenham, Chelsea, Aston Villa. Plays and musical revues were also put on in this large subcamp, and for further amusement Les and his mates took every opportunity to bait the 'goons', confusing the Germans during rollcall, pouring water down the chimney of the guardhouse (*Kommandantur*), distilling hooch disguised as 'dirty washing'. As the war ground to its close, the guards, now elderly, were treated as an even greater joke, with at least one trip to a bar, and a date arranged in German with a pretty girl en route back to the camp. The prisoners knew the end was in sight.

'Aston Villa' – one of the many named football teams at the large workcamp (*Arbeitskommando*) E1 at Laband, administered by Stalag VIIIB. Football kits were supplied by the Red Cross, boots by the YMCA. Leslie Doyle is second from the left on the back row. The men are posing in front of the wire fence, but the barbed wire has been blanked out by the Germans during processing.

ASTON-VILLA

Les Doyle's medals. Typical of most British prisoners of war captured in 1940, he would receive only two campaign medals for his five years of endurance – the War Medal and 1939–45 Star.

The threat to the Germans of the advancing Soviet army meant that the prisoners moved out of the camp on 22 January 1945, with little food and in the grip of a central European winter. As they marched westwards in stages, enduring starvation (mangels taken from the roadside being often the only food), intense cold and frostbite, many of Les Doyle's mates fell by the wayside to be severely dealt with by the German guards. Then one day, after three months of marching, the guards melted away and the Americans appeared. Given ample food, Les and his mates were billeted on a terrified German family; fear was dispelled by an act of basic humanity – sharing the food with the hungry family. In May 1945, Les was flown back to England in a Lancaster bomber.

He never forgot what had happened to him.

PRIVATE ABEN S. CAPLEN, KRIEGSGEFANGENER 145166, STALAG VIIA

Aben Caplen was a Jewish boy from Chicago, an able soldier serving with the 3rd Infantry Division when it entered the European Theater of Operations (ETO) on 9 July 1943. The 3rd had joined the war a year earlier, when it had taken part in the Allied landings on the coast of North Africa, fighting the Vichy French, and it went on to aid in the defeat of Axis forces in the region, a task finally completed in May 1943. The amphibious invasions of Sicily, and then mainland Italy, were to follow in quick succession – the 3rd taking part in the landings at Anzio in January 1944. Sergeant Caplen took part in his final amphibious landing – that of the invasion of southern France – on 15 August 1944, and was at the spearhead of the invasion, part of the US 7th Army that would sweep (with General Patton's 3rd Army) the Germans before them, finally reaching the Rhine in the Alsace region of France in the fall of that year. Here, the 7th Army waited to cross the Rhine for four months, soldiers like Aben Caplen regularly patrolling and raiding the German forces on the other side, held on the defensive while Hitler's last offensive in the Ardennes tried in vain to punch a hole in the Allies' lines farther north.

Private Caplen's military service took a surprising turn on 24 January 1945 as he joined in the active patrols on the Rhine, in a raid that was intended to secure a small creek so that it could be bridged, thereby allowing armour to come up in support. Company I led the attack under the cover of

Shoulder patch and rank badges of a Technical Sergeant of the US 3rd Infantry Division – Aben Caplen's division and eventual rank.

darkness. With a little knowledge of German, Aben interrogated a German POW, little expecting that he himself would soon become a captive. A fierce German counterattack – supported by heavy tanks – had the company diving for cover and it was not long before Aben and his men were captured: it was either that or be crushed under the weight of a German tank heading directly for his foxhole. He later wrote: 'At that moment we became prisoners of war as we came out of our hole, hands held overhead, all weapons removed, and all our equipment and packs left strewn all around as we were quickly herded together and rapidly marched off to Jerries [sic] lines.' As with all POWs, the rapidity of his capture took him by surprise: 'The thought of becoming a prisoner of war had never previously entered my mind. It's impossible to adequately express how depressed I felt at that time.'

Even at this late stage, the Germans were vigorously prosecuting the war, heartened by the early successes in the Ardennes Offensive to the north, and these men captured on the Rhine were a large influx of American POWs that had to be moved out of the battle zone as quickly as possible. In common with all new captives, Aben Caplen was marched eastwards to take up residence in a permanent stalag. At an early stage of his capture, Aben knew that his religion could become an issue; fearing for his long-term safety, he nevertheless kept hold of a prayer book that had been a comfort to him in the minutes before capture, a decision he never regretted. From Command Post to headquarters, Private Caplen and his men were passed back through the German lines, with watches, wallets and other personal effects being taken by the Germans. Aben acted as interpreter when the men were faced with interrogation but only the usual details were forthcoming from the Americans.

As it was for most POWs, transit to the permanent camp was a trying experience. Marched for days and fed the usual soup and bread, the men became hungry. Tempers frayed and fights broke out over the division of issue. Intermittently marching and boarding rail cattle trucks, they passed through transit camps (such as Stalag VA, Ludwigsburg) and cities such as Freiburg and Stuttgart, where the American soldiers saw for themselves the destruction wrought by the Allied strategic bombing campaign. Finally, on 4 March 1945, Aben Caplen's long journey into captivity ended, at Stalag VIIA, Moosburg, Bavaria.

Stalag VIIA was the largest POW camp in Germany, a standard hutted camp near Munich, with over 130,000 prisoners from twenty-six countries on its roster. It was also to house the largest number of American prisoners, 30,000, captured mostly in the Ardennes. Later, it would serve as a transit camp for the men from Stalag Luft III on their long march westwards. On arrival Aben and his comrades were deloused, shaved, registered as POWs, issued with identity discs and separated into compounds. Filled beyond

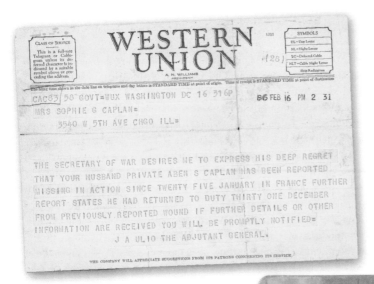

Above: Western Union telegram reporting that Private Aben Caplen was missing in action, January 1945. (Library of Congress)

Right: Aben Caplen's *Kriegsgefangener* identity disc. (Library of Congress)

Below: Aben's postcard home to Chicago from Stalag VIIA, Moosburg. (Library of Congress)

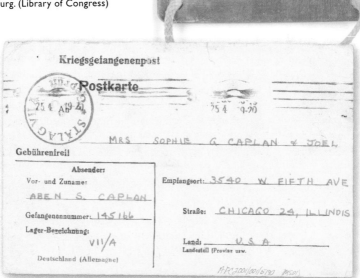

PRISONER OF WAR IN GERMANY

capacity, the huts did not have enough bunks to accommodate the men, who had to sleep on tables and the floor. The prisoners were grateful for their Red Cross parcels, and Aben saw merits in all he received – from US, British and Canadian Red Cross sources. Identified as Jewish, Aben and many others were picked out from the main body of men to be housed in a separate compound – an action that provoked vociferous complaints to the Swiss Protecting Power from the American 'Man of Confidence'. There were no further such actions.

The men were forced to work, on *Arbeitskommandos* near Munich, and Aben as interpreter and hut leader helped supervise his men, ensuring they did as little as possible. They worked on the railways, which was a hazardous experience, with Allied aircraft continually searching for targets. Aben and his buddies had to paint POW in large letters on the roofs of their accommodation and hope for the best.

After being a prisoner for just over three months, Private Caplen was freed by his countrymen, on 30 April 1945. They were liberated by the men of the US 13th Armored Division, whose tanks were met by a hand-made American flag that Aben had designed in the camp.

Finally free, Aben never forgot the strength he had received from his prayer book, and from the knowledge that his wife and child in Chicago, Illinois, were awaiting his return.

Western Union telegram reporting Private Aben Caplen liberated, April 1945. (Library of Congress)

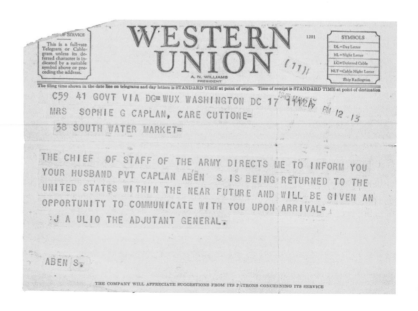

Handley Page Halifax, a four-engined heavy bomber, one of the workhorses of the RAF's strategic bombing campaign: this example is a Mark III. Flying Officer Duncan Black was one of the eight-man crew of a Mark II version, shot down by ground flak over the Ruhr on the night of 11–12 June 1943.

FLYING OFFICER DUNCAN BLACK RAF, KRIEGSGEFANGENER 1488, STALAG LUFT III

Flying Officer Black was a Scot. Born in Edinburgh to a middle-class family, he was well educated and training to be an architect. Like so many other young men, he joined the Royal Air Force through its Volunteer Reserve (VR), and was trained as an RAF navigator to help guide the bombers taking the war deep into the heart of Germany. By the end of the war the vast majority of Bomber Command aircrew had come through the RAFVR. Fully trained, Duncan Black was posted to 419 Squadron, a mostly Canadian unit forming part of 6 Group Bomber Command. The squadron was based at RAF Middleton St George in County Durham, northern England, and by 1943 was flying four-engined Halifax bombers. The squadron was an integral part of the RAF's strategic night-bombing campaign of Germany, designed to knock out the engineering potential of Germany, and to dampen the will of the German people to carry on their fight.

Between March and July 1943, Bomber Command was attacking the industrial heartland of Germany, the Ruhr. Duncan Black's aircraft, Halifax JD 143 VR-A, piloted by FO W. J. Boyce of the Royal Canadian Air Force, formed part of an 800-bomber raid on the city of Düsseldorf. It took off from Middleton St George at 2240hrs on the night of 11 June 1943, never to return – one of forty aircraft from that raid alone. The aircraft was hit by flak as it approached the Ruhr; FO Black never forgot the actions of his pilot. He later wrote from Dulag Luft: 'Bill I think, is dead. He died saving the lives of the crew, holding the stricken aircraft until we were safely away.' Five of the eight-man crew survived to become prisoners of war – and members of the exclusive 'Caterpillar Club', aircrew saved by parachute from stricken aircraft.

Duncan Black's first letter home (dated July 1943) from the interrogation centre for air-force prisoners – Dulag Luft, near Frankfurt am Main. The letter describes his crash, and his resignation to POW life.

All five were picked up by the local police west of Duisburg. As Duncan had received a wound in the raid, evading capture – perhaps using the compasses and silk maps provided to all airmen – was not a serious option.

As the Luftwaffe jealously guarded its responsibility for RAF and USAAF personnel, Duncan Black and his comrades were quickly handed over to them from the civil and military authorities, travelling by train to the main interrogation centre, Dulag Luft, on the outskirts of Frankfurt am Main. Here, the usual ploys were tried in order to gain information; put in solitary confinement, Duncan received bogus Red Cross forms to fill in with details of his unit and aircraft. Fortunately the Allied air forces were well aware of these ploys, and had fully briefed their personnel. He supplied only the traditional name, rank and serial number to his interrogators. After a few days FO Black was passed for transit to his main camp, Stalag Luft III at Sagan in Silesia.

Stalag Luft III was one of the most important air-force POW camps in Germany. Initiated in October 1942, it grew in stages, with additional

Kriegsgefangener identity disc from Stalag Luft III, similar to that worn by Duncan Black in captivity.

and separate compounds constructed over time. It was situated in a fresh clearing in the dense East European pine forest so that the trees blocked out the light, while the sounds of the rail marshalling yards of Sagan Station in the distance tempted the prisoners to dream of escape. The camp would eventually house 10,000 Allied airmen, at first in what became known as the Centre (for NCOs) and East (for officers) Compounds, followed by North, South and West Compounds as more and more Allied flyers arrived. Each compound was surrounded by the usual double-wire fence watched over by 'goon boxes', the huts themselves raised up on stilts to discourage tunnelling – which was in itself a difficult proposition given the distinctiveness of the bright yellow subsoil, notoriously hard to disguise. The huts were equipped with washrooms, and were divided into rooms housing around ten men in double bunks. The *Vorlager*, containing guardhouse, 'hospital' and 'cooler', completed the setup.

The remains of one of the huts today, in the former North Compound of Stalag Luft III at Sagan (now Zagan, in Poland). The camp has returned to forest.

Like many captured in 1943, Duncan Black found his way into the East Compound, scene of the highly successful 'Wooden Horse' escape of the same year, before being moved to the newly constructed North Compound, which has gained even greater notoriety as the setting of the 'Great Escape' in March 1944. The move provided Duncan with plenty of opportunity to develop his skills. As an officer and trained airman, working outside the camp was not possible, and all his activities were focused on developing a life inside the barbed wire. He continued the study of architecture, and found an outlet for his skills in the design of the new theatre in the North Compound. He also designed sets for theatrical productions including such Shakespearean standards as *A Midsummer Night's Dream* and *As You Like It*, tried his hand as a

watercolourist (materials supplied from home), and engaged in conversational French with Belgian members of the RAF.

As work was forbidden all prisoners of Stalag Luft III, monotony was a constant and universal theme; and while some would engage in escape activity (estimated at around 30 per cent of the camp at any one time), most would make the best of a bad job. Duncan Black would describe the burden of time in a letter home in 1943:

We get up about 9, have breakfast, go out on parade, wash up, spend the rest of the morning in divers ways (there is the education scheme, the theatre, the rugby field, the wash-house) to interest one, or perhaps walk around the outside of our little patch of Germany. That takes about seven minutes. Then lunch, more washing-up (really this washing racket is a bind), the afternoon (very like the morning) tea, parade, evening (much as the afternoon).

Above:
One of Duncan
Black's books used
in Stalag Luft III.

Below: Remains of the camp theatre, built by prisoners at Stalag Luft III. Duncan Black was the architect for this construction.

Duncan found time to reflect on the community of prisoners:

> This life is a constant source of wonder to me. That a perfectly civilised and
> rational community, *sans* women, having as it does all the more important
> amenities of the outside world, can be run without money or motor cars,
> shops or washing machines, is a feat worth considering. My interests are
> many and varied and it would not be possible to set them all down on paper,
> but the barbed wire barricades are not of great importance.

In common with all kriegies in Silesia, Duncan Black and his comrades found
his escape in the last desperate march westwards, when the camp was
evacuated on 27 January 1945. They had a long march in sub-zero
temperatures, before finally being liberated in April 1945.

Collection of
letters describing
life in Stalag Luft
III, sent home from
the camp by
Duncan Black.

ESCAPE AND LIBERATION

FOR a generation brought up on films such as *The Great Escape*, *The Colditz Story*, and *The Wooden Horse*, the perception of kriegie life is one of enforced idleness, incarcerated behind barbed wire fences, ever looking for an opportunity to escape. Although often stated that 'it was a prisoner's duty to escape' – now embedded in POW mythology – the reality was somewhat different. According to Squadron Leader B. A. 'Jimmy' James, veteran of several attempts, including the famed 'Great Escape' of March 1944, within one camp alone, Stalag Luft III, there were to be three main kriegie 'types': hardened escaper, POWs willing to assist in escapes, and those committed to 'seeing out the war', come what may.

Achieving a 'home run' – getting back to Allied territory – was the ultimate aim of any escaper. The factors controlling escape and the desire to escape were varied. In camps for officers and air-force personnel (as well as Stalag 383, the *Sonderlager* for non-working NCOs) life could be one of unrelenting monotony. RAF Sergeant Bill Critchley of Stalag Luft III would put it succinctly in 1942: 'I manage to keep pretty cheerful, but the monotony and inactivity is hellish.' Often well educated and highly trained, with energy and enthusiasm to spare, these men could plot escape. For most men in the stalags, obliged to work six days out of seven on a diet that barely kept life and limb together, escape was hardly a practical proposition. What's more, many of these camps were situated deliberately in the eastern part of the Reich territory, hundreds of miles away from neutral countries such as Switzerland or Sweden, or British territories such as Gibraltar.

Escape from most POW camps required ingenuity, luck, hard work and planning. Tunnelling out is seen as a classic form of escape, and it was attempted in most camps. The success of tunnelling was at the mercy of the ground conditions as well as the vigilance of the security staff, and was a test of ingenuity. In some cases, escapers were lucky to have men with expertise. Lt Jim Rogers of the Royal Engineers was one such man, a tunnelling engineer by profession; he was to end up in Oflag IVC, Colditz Castle (the notorious 'bad boys' camp'), following his failed attempt at a tunnelled escape

Opposite:
Kriegie literature. Prisoner of war books, written mostly by ex-kriegies, were extremely popular in the immediate post-war era. Most of them centred on escape adventures; only a few concentrated on endurance.

Below left: The
inner courtyard of
Colditz Castle (the
former Oflag IVC)
today.

Below right:
Looking down into
the French tunnel
cut through the
solid rock
underneath Colditz
Castle. The tunnel
started in the clock
tower, and cut
through various
foundations. It was
discovered before a
hole was breached
in the outer wall on
15 January 1942
after many months
of activity.

in 1941 from Oflag VIIC at Laufen, Bavaria. Another was Pilot Officer 'Wally' Floody, a Canadian aviator who had spent part of his youth as a miner in Ontario, and was the man instrumental in designing the 'Great Escape' tunnels in 1944. Finding a means to dig through the surface undetected, combating the ground conditions – whether the tough volcanic rocks of Colditz or the soft yellow sands of Stalag Luft III, and then successfully disposing of the waste, were major preoccupations for these men.

For their part, the Germans were not minded to sit back and wait while tunnelling took place; instead, specially trained security officers – usually referred to as 'ferrets' after their ability to 'sniff out' a tunnel – were detailed to investigate any suspicious activities. The sub-surface yellow sands of Stalag Luft III were a particular giveaway when spilled on the grey surface soils of the camp. Anti-tunnelling measures, such as building huts on raised piers, and the use of buried listening devices, were also prevalent. It is not surprising therefore that in air-force camps alone, only one in thirty-five escape tunnels was successful.

The most famous tunnel escapes, those that have passed into legend, include the shallow tunnel constructed under a wooden vaulting horse (the

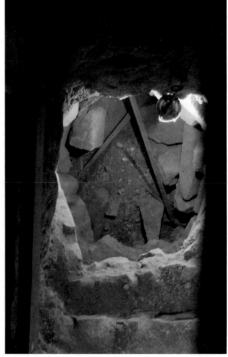

The shaft 30 feet deep to 'Harry', the escape tunnel operated by the prisoners of Stalag Luft III on the night of 24 March 1944. Seventy-six prisoners got out of the tunnel; three made 'home-runs', twenty-three were returned to the camp, fifty were murdered, in ones and twos, by the Gestapo. (IWM HU 21228)

'Wooden Horse') in the East Compound of Stalag Luft III in 1943 (100 per cent successful, with three home runs); and the 'Great Escape' of March 1944, in which three 30-foot-deep tunnels were dug in 1943–4. One of them, 'Harry', was operated on the evening of 23 March 1944, with seventy-six men emerging into the night; three got home, twenty-three were sent back to the camp, and fifty murdered, in ones and twos, by the Gestapo. There were many other, less celebrated, tunnel escapes.

Other escape methods included attacking the wire, either by vaulting over it or by cutting through it. This was an extremely risky business, given the vigilance of the machine-gun armed guards within the 'goon towers'. The 'Warburg Wire Job' of August 1942 was particularly audacious, with forty-one

Archaeologist working on tunnel 'Dick', one of the 'Great Escape' tunnels at Stalag Luft III, during the author's archaeological investigations in 2003; the airline made by the 'tin-bashers' and remains of the wooden bed-board supports can be made out in the distinctive yellow sands.

Above left: Squadron Leader B. A. 'Jimmy' James and Flight Lieutenant Sydney Dowse, two of the 'Great Escapers' of March 1944, pictured in 2004. Both got free of the tunnel but were recaptured and were lucky not to be shot by the Gestapo. They would, however, end up in a *Sonderlager* for escapees at Sachsenhausen Concentration Camp – from where they escaped, only to be re-caught.

Above right: Memorial to the fifty men murdered by the Gestapo following the Great Escape from Stalag Luft III in March 1944. The memorial was constructed by the prisoners themselves.

Right: Gravel path marking the position of the escape tunnel 'Harry' at Stalag Luft III, from which seventy-six escapers emerged on the night of 24 March 1944.

prisoners escaping over the wire at Oflag VIB through the use of three hinged ladders. Three men made home runs, though at the heavy price of one man electrocuted cutting through the cables to the lights illuminating the wire.

For prison camps located in the medieval castles of Germany, pluck was the most important prerequisite, and walking through the camp gates was often the only way out. This was tried at other camps too; celebrated was the attempt by naval officer Lt D. P. James, who slipped away from Marlag-Milag Nord in December 1943 dressed in full British naval uniform, adopting the fake identity of 'Lt I. Bagerov' of the 'Royal Bulgarian Navy'; a dummy stood in for him at rollcall. Despite the eccentric brilliance of his plan, it failed, with him getting only as far as the dock gates at Lübeck before being discovered.

For most committed escapers, transfer to one particular destination would be expected: Oflag IVC Colditz, a forbidding castle considered by some to be 'escape proof'. Thirty-two men from five nationalities tested that theory, with fifteen home runs recorded, the first British home run being that of Lt Airey Neave, who walked out of the camp dressed as a German officer on 5 January 1942.

The value of returned POWs, both in terms of experience of the internal workings of the Third Reich, and of the return of valuable and well-trained service personnel, was not lost on the British and American governments, both of which developed secret branches of their intelligence services both to assist in escape and to take part in the debriefing of returned POWs. These organisations – MI9 and MIS-X – were instrumental in designing a wide range of escape equipment. This was sent to POWs through international channels, secreted in materials other than food (so as not to jeopardise the supply of this most important resource), such as Monopoly sets, playing cards

Air vent in the outer wall of Colditz Castle (Oflag IVC), through which four prisoners, including Captain Pat Reid, escaped on 15 October 1942. All succeeded in making 'home runs' from this vent, which was in the *Kommandantur* – the camp garrison.

Hole in the ceiling of Colditz Castle through which Lt Airey Neave made his escape on 5 January 1942. The hole led from beneath the theatre into the guardhouse. Neave walked through the gate dressed as a German officer, and made it home to England.

and gramophone records. Maps and compasses designed by these organisations also became standard for aircrew flying over Germany, sewn into flying suits and secreted in buttons.

Prisoners also manufactured their own escape equipment: compasses from razor blades and gramophone records (forming the cases), forger's stamps from rubber boot heels, and maps reproduced using gelatin as a printing medium. All were vital – together with forged papers, sufficient food and a good knowledge of German – if the hope of a home run was to be realistic.

For those recaptured, the maximum punishment as defined by the Geneva Convention was thirty days in solitary confinement within

Maps hidden inside playing cards supplied to prisoners in Stalag Luft III, Sagan, by the MI9 and MIS-X organisations. (IWM HU 21199)

Above: Wehrmacht stamp forged by prisoners from a rubber boot heel, intricately cut out using razor blades. This vital piece of equipment was used in forging escape papers, and was found in the shaft of 'Dick', one of the 'Great Escape' tunnels, during the author's archaeological investigations at Stalag Luft III in 2003.

Left: Air-force escape and evasion aids, including a silk escape map, small compass points designed to be sewn into uniforms, and a specially magnetised razor blade designed by MI9/MIS-X to be used in the manufacture of escape compasses. Escape maps were made from silk to reduce the rustling sound of standard maps.

punishment cells – famously called 'coolers' or 'bunkers' by prisoners and guards alike. Others, such as the fifty murdered by the Gestapo after the 'Great Escape', would not be as fortunate.

For sick, wounded and maimed soldiers, there was hope of repatriation, a principle that formed part of the Geneva Convention. For seriously injured men, the first hopes of repatriation came in 1941, when 1,153 prisoners were passed by a medical commission (comprising doctors from Germany and two neutral countries). These hopes were dashed even as the men were on their way to a special repatriation camp at Rouen, when the scheme was cancelled over a dispute about the number of able-bodied medical orderlies to be returned with these men. The prisoners were returned, crestfallen, to their original camps. In the aftermath of the Dieppe shackling incident, new negotiations took time to organise, but by 1943 the first tranche of 5,000 British, Commonwealth and American men was repatriated via Sweden, with three other tranches between May 1944 and January 1945 amounting to some 6,000 or more prisoners. Some kriegies tried to 'work the system' to gain repatriation; madness was feigned, and in one celebrated example RAF Sergeant Richard Pape used a false penis in order to pass nephritis-infected urine (harvested from a fellow prisoner) and thereby earn his repatriation from Stalag Luft VI in September 1944.

For those not lucky enough to be considered for repatriation, and not committed enough to engage directly in escape activities, there was nothing left but to 'see out the war'. With Red Cross parcels to sustain life, and activities to refresh mind and soul, endurance became the mindset. Hopes of an early Allied victory following D-Day in June 1944 — reports snatched from the BBC on radio sets bartered from the guards for chocolate and cigarettes — were quickly ground down, as the Western Allies met stiff resistance. The capture of 6,000 airborne soldiers after Arnhem in September 1944 and 27,500 American troops in the Ardennes in December of the same year did little to raise spirits. Rapidly collapsing German resistance in the East gave some hope in 1945, but with this came the collapse of the supply chain for Red Cross parcels, and the return to the hunger felt by those who had first entered the camps in June 1940. Only the determination of the White Angels of the International Red Cross kept men from real starvation.

For the Germans, the worsening military situation in the east posed them real difficulties. Should the men of the camps be abandoned to the 'Bolshevik hordes', or should they be

YMCA logbook kept by Captain Müller MC of the New Zealand Army Service Corps at Oflag IXA/Z, Rotenburg, recording the day of liberation by American forces, on Friday 13 April 1945.

marched westwards in order to act as a bargaining counter in the final battles for the Reich? The 'Long March' took thousands of Allied POWs from Silesia and the eastern Reich, marching 300–500 miles across Germany from camp to camp. They travelled with minimum rations, in freezing temperatures and with increasing brutality from their guards. The men resorted once more to scavenging for food but even so many died from the combination of physical weakness, exposure and the random viciousness of their captors. Others were mentally scarred and physically debilitated for life from this experience. Allied aircraft, masters of German airspace, would also unknowingly strafe their own men – who became unwitting victims in the battle for Germany. But one day, when the German guards melted away.

Liberation when it came took many forms. For some camps, such as Stalag Luft I at Barth, on the Baltic coast, liberation was by the advancing Russians, the evacuation of Barth having been left too late. For many others, it was the Americans. At Colditz, the prisoners watched with horror as a pitched battle was fought with SS Hitler Youth troops at the base of the castle walls. Finding flags flying from the walls, the bewildered GI who entered the castle was mobbed by the gaunt men waiting for their freedom. Such scenes were repeated the length and breadth of defeated Germany.

Returning home as soon as possible was the priority of all ex-kriegies, who in many cases were corralled in altogether more civilised conditions in transit camps awaiting their freedom. Debriefed by members of MI9 and MIS-X, some prisoners had opportunity to report on atrocity and collaboration, but for most this debriefing was a formality. For Britons, repatriation was often by air, ferried by the pilots of Bomber and Transport Commands as aircraft became available, part of Operation *Exodus*. North Americans and Australasians, equally anxious to return but from more distant lands, embarked on ships. For all, rehabilitation took time, with readjustment from the quirks of kriegie life and from the starvation diet of the latter days of the war the first necessities.

HINTS ON DIET DURING RECUPERATIVE LEAVE FOR LIBERATED PRISONERS OF WAR

As a result of the privations you have endured as a prisoner of war, you have probably lost weight, and it is natural to think that the more food you eat the sooner will you recover your lost weight and strength. But you must remember that your physique as well as your weight may be temporarily below par, and this includes your digestive system. Just as you need rest at first and your muscles require gradual retraining, so your digestive system requires rest at first and then retraining in the handling of the sort of foods you normally like to eat.

To get your digestive system back to normal as quickly as possible, a few simple rules that you should follow, especially if you are having trouble with your digestion, are given in the dietetic instructions below. You should show these notes and the following instructions to anyone who is giving you your meals, so that they can understand why you have to be careful about eating for a time, and what they should give you to eat.

(1) **Don't overload your stomach.** Avoid heavy meals, and instead, eat small amounts frequently. Try eating three light meals a day, with three snacks of the biscuits and milk variety —two between meals and one last thing at night.

(2) **Remember that your digestion is weak, and at first give your stomach foods easy to handle.**

Eat : Foods such as milk and milk puddings, eggs, cereals, toast or bread, biscuits, preserves, cake, and fish and tender meat if you can eat these without discomfort.

Avoid at first : Fatty or fried foods, bulky vegetables, raw salads or fruit, highly seasoned dishes, twice-cooked meats, pickles and spices, rich, heavy puddings and pastries, strong tea and coffee.

Beer and other alcoholic drinks are hard on a weak stomach, and you should take these very sparingly, if at all, for the first few days at least.

'Hints on Diet during Recuperative Leave for Returned Prisoners of War'. After many months of a near-starvation diet, POWs took some time to adjust to the balanced meals served at home.

SUGGESTED READING

The books recommended below provide a range of further reading. Very many prisoner of war memoirs were published in the aftermath of the war, and although many are out of print, they are worth reading if encountered in second-hand bookshops. There are many more than are listed here. There are also very many valuable web resources, including detailed accounts of prisoners' experiences in the US Library of Congress Veterans History Project (www.loc.gov/vets/stories/pow-germany.html).

OVERVIEW

Bowman, M.W. (1987) *Home by Christmas: Story of US 8th/15th Air Force Airmen at War*. Patrick Stephens, London.

Foy, D. A. (1984) *For You the War is Over: American Prisoners of War in Nazi Germany*. Stein & Day, New York.

Gilbert, A. (2006) *POW. Allied Prisoners in Europe, 1939–1945*. John Murray, London.

Mackenzie, S. P. (2004) *The Colditz Myth. British and Commonwealth Prisoners of War in Nazi Germany*. Oxford University Press.

Nichol, J., and Rennell, T. (2002) *The Last Escape. The Untold Story of Allied Prisoners of War in Germany 1944–45*. Viking, London.

Reid, P., and Michael, M. (1984) *Prisoner of War*. Hamlyn, London.

PRISONER MEMOIRS

Anderson, R., and Westmacott, D. (1946) *Handle with Care. A Book of Prison Camp Sketches*. Privately Published.

Arct, B. (1988) *Prisoner of War. My Secret Journal*. Webb & Bower, Exeter.

Belson, D. (2003) *Caught! Prisoner of War No. 487*. Bentwyck Henry, Henley-on-Thames.

Edgar, D. (1982) *The Stalag Men*. John Clare Books, London.

Graham, J., and Thomas, J. (1946) *Joe in Germany*. Surrey Fine Art Press, Redhill.

Mackay, A. (1998) *313 Days to Christmas*. Argyll Publishing, Glendaruel.

McKibbin, M. N., and Dallimore, A.G. (1946) *Barbed Wire. Memories of Stalag 383*. Staples Press, London.

Morgan, G. (1945) *Only Ghosts Can Live*. Crosby Lockwood, London.

Prouse, A. R. (1982) *Ticket to Hell Via Dieppe*. Webb & Bower, Exeter.

Rogers, J. (1986) *Tunnelling into Colditz*. Robert Hale, London.

Sabey, I. (1947) *Stalag Scrapbook*. F. W. Cheshire, Melbourne.

Vincent, A. (1956) *The Long Road Home*. George Allen & Unwin, London.

Williamson, L. (1988) *Six Wasted Years*. Merlin Books, Braunton.

ESCAPE ACCOUNTS

Brickhill, P. (1951) *The Great Escape*. Faber & Faber, London.

Chancellor, H. (2001) *Colditz*. Hodder & Stoughton, London.

Crawley, A. (1956) *Escape from Germany. A History of R.A.F. Escapes during the War*. Collins, London.

Dunning, G. (1955) *Where Bleed the Many*. Elek, London.

Evans, A. J. (1945) *Escape and Liberation, 1940–1945*. Hodder & Stoughton, London.

Foot, M. R. D., and Langley, J. M. (1979) *MI9 Escape and Evasion 1939–1945*. The Bodley Head, London.

James, B. A. (2001) *Moonless Night*. Leo Cooper, Barnsley

Pape, R. (1953) *Boldness Be My Friend*. Elek, London.

Reid, P. (1952) *The Colditz Story*. Hodder & Stoughton, London.

Vance, J. F. (2000) *A Gallant Company. Men of the Great Escape*. Ibooks, New York.

Williams, E. (1949) *The Wooden Horse*. Collins, London.

Williams, E. (1951) *The Tunnel*. Collins, London.

OTHER

Baybut, R. (1982) *Camera in Colditz*. Hodder & Stoughton, London.

Bookes, M. (2005) *Collecting Colditz and its Secrets*. Grub Street, London.

Swallow, T., and Pill, A. H. (1987) *Flywheel. Memories of the Open Road*. Webb & Bower, Exeter.

INDEX